WHAT WE
ASK
OF FLESH

Also by Remica L. Bingham

Conversion (Lotus Press, 2007)
Winner of the Naomi Long Madgett Poetry Award

WHAT WE
ASK
OF FLESH

poems

REMICA L.
BINGHAM

etruscan press

Etruscan Press
Wilkes University
84 West South Street
Wilkes-Barre, PA 18766
(570) 408-4546

www.etruscanpress.org

Published 2013 by Etruscan Press
Printed in the United States of America
Cover and author photo © Rachel Eliza Griffiths
www.rachele,lizagriffiths.com
Design by Julianne Popovec
The text of this book is set in Adobe Garamond Pro.

First Edition

13 14 15 16 17 5 4 3 2 1

Library of Congress Cataloguing-in-Publication Data

[copy and paste CIP for this book here]

Please turn to the back of this book for a list of the sustaining funders of Etruscan Press.

This book is printed on recycled, acid-free paper.

For Mary E. Knight,
who always taught us
The truth is the light

tell yourself that anytime now
we will rise and walk away
from somebody else's life
                    —Lucille Clifton

WHAT WE ASK OF FLESH

Acknowledgments

Grateful acknowledgment is given to following publications where some of these poems first appeared, sometimes in different versions or under different titles:

"All the Wild Swarm" and "Something Divine Let Go," *Callaloo;* "The Body Speaks [First section—*we become what we live* . . .], [Second section—*There is no such work* . . .] and [Fifth section—*Say vulva and make it clean* . . .]," *Toad;* "The Body Speaks [Third section—*My milk was sweet and dark* . . .]," *Harvard Review;* "How I Crossed Over," *phati'tude;* "Maieusiophobia," *Ars Medica;* "Things I Carried Coming Into the World," *PMS (poemmemoirstory)*; "What We Ask of Flesh [Section I.—*IMPORTANT SAFEGUARDS* . . .], [Section II.—*The girl does not smile* . . .] and [Section V.—*She coats her new skin* . . .]," *Connotations Press: An Online Artifact;* and "Will and Testament," *Mythium.*

All praise to Jehovah God for inspiring Matthew 26:41: "The spirit, of course, is eager, but the flesh is weak . . . " And for the promise at Acts 2:26: "On this account my heart became cheerful and my tongue rejoiced greatly. Moreover, even my flesh will reside in hope . . . "

All my love to my family, the Bingham, Knight, Anderson clans, and all other extended beauties. Especially for their encouragement in all its forms, my love to: Doris and Robert Bingham, Alesia Anderson, Radeem Ellington, Rosalind Bingham-Ellington, Uncle Charlie Wise, Deborah Bingham, Kalani Dozier (whose spirit is here in many manifestations), Randy Bingham Jr. (for always questioning), Shirley Bingham, Julius Bingham, and Loretta Bingham. To all my babies: Jasmin, Rashad, Nicole, Shavon, Johnathan, Sonsoréa, and Michael, for patience. To my husband, Michael Risher, who reminds me everyday that passion is a gift.

So many friends and mentors have helped bring this book to light: Matilda Cox and Princess J. L. Perry (for every waking moment), Eugene Calloway, Honorée Fanonne Jeffers, Myron Michael Hardy, James Cagney, Dante Micheaux, Frank X. Walker, Jericho Brown, Christian Campbell, L. Lamar Wilson, John Murillo, Patricia Biela (who told me I was a rockstar when I needed to hear it), Reginald Dwayne Betts, DeLana Dameron,

Amanda Johnston, Christina Archer, Phillip Williams, Jeannie and Travis Kim-McPherson (for melody and harmony), Anita Darcel Taylor, Ada Udechukwu, Christal Brown and INSPIRIT (who make words dance), CC '06 Group D and the wide net that is Cave Canem, Alison Meyers, Anastacia Tolbert, Randall Horton, Rachel Eliza Griffiths (for always seeing), Camille Dungy, Nikki Giovanni, Kwame Dawes, and Patricia Smith.

A special thank you to Philip Brady for his enduring confidence in this work, to Starr Troup for all the details, and to the entire Etruscan staff for all of their care.

To all those who continually sustain me: light and love.

Introduction

There aren't many real colored girls left.

Not sistas. Not "women of color," not African-American females, not black women. There are thousands upon thousands of those, raising their voices, beautifying what surrounds them.

Colored girls.

What's increasingly rare these days is the girl still harboring a hard knot of doubledutch in her calves. The girl who won't wear pants to church *no matter what you say*, who still prefers a sizzling hot comb over a perm. She misses her patent leather Mary Janes and the Saturday morning chittlin' assembly line. She loves her mama and her man, cooks all day on Sunday, praises Jesus.

No matter how old the colored girl is, she dances, knows where her hips are and what they're equipped to do. She still rocks the Cabbage Patch, and well. She gravitates toward the addictive sugar of soul music, follows the gospel of Smokey and the Temps until she realizes how gorgeous their lies were. Shamelessly off key, she sings everything from hymns to commercial jingles, with her sound cranked way up and the windows thrown wide open. She doesn't care who hears her.

The colored girl is undeniably rooted in a world that fits her perfectly, and has long ago stopped apologizing for—well, anything. She is the sole crafter of her own story, a story which is both comfortable and insistently evolving. And when she feels that it is time to tell that story, unbridled and aloud, the air shifts restlessly around her. For those moments, she is everyone, no one. God stands behind and beside her. Her life blazes.

A fervent song of praise is threaded through these stanzas. The mistress Bingham praises with her head thrown back, wailing to the rafters, then whispering in the back row of the choir. Colored girls know one thing more than they know anything else, and that is that a God is real and present, hurtling through our blood, blessing us every dawn with a blank canvas upon which to sing. *Who sent us/ forward/ or back?* These poems move purposely toward a light that shines for anyone who reads them.

Remica Bingham is, undoubtedly, a colored girl, one of a disappearing breed. And her story—which she unreels here in deftly-crafted stanzas, lean and lyrical—is oft-told, but never this way. Her voice rises, sole and singular, above the fray as she conjures a soundtrack for the wife, the mother, the sister, the daughter, the colored girl who has quietly persevered while resisting attempts to change her beliefs, her history, her environment, even the contours of her body. The poems in the pages shimmer with assurance, spinning a complicated world out loud while holding fast to old-school sensibilities that both spice and sweeten the mix.

"There is no such work," the poet says, "as a woman's. . . ." Boldly she begins by giving voice to the body, defining and celebrating its frailties and fists, its honey hue. *Say vulva. Say labia. Not cyst. Say slide. They scrape. They rip. They scourge.* The poet celebrates our "miraculous scars." She admits that we are "tethered to this life by what's missing." Then she reveals to us, in no uncertain terms, just what is missing. The layers peel away to reveal so much—a story beneath the stories, a spiritual groundwork from the Book of Judges, but if it is your story you see, that is the story you will see.

She leaves the body to enter the circle of family, and she is unflinching in her place among them, in her description of the landscape of "my family's back," she refuses to turn away from what doesn't conform. Her focus on the frailties and gifts of family is camera-tight, revelatory. The colored girl looks hard at where she comes from, wrapping her arms around tragedy and pulling it close. She puts scars on display, reveals wounds, and bellows triumph throughout.

And the close of this book simply stuns, as the poet sends three wondrous colored girls—the poets Lucille Clifton, Ai, and Carolyn Rodgers—gently into their deaths with swift elegies that resound long after their breathless final lines.

It seems anticlimactic to speak of craft, because here it's so seamless and ingrained. There is innovation, building upon and blooming from the words of other women; there are both traditional and freshly-birthed rhythms living in the lines.

Because that's what colored girls do. They find new things in order to own them. They revel in what is believed in, what has always been there. And then they open their mouths to sing a song with mingled notes of hurt and hallelujah. It's a song fewer and fewer women know how to sing.

Open this book. And listen.

—PATRICIA SMITH, Author of *Blood Dazzler*
and *Teahouse of the Almighty*

WHAT WE
ASK
OF FLESH

THE BODY SPEAKS

"Then he entered his house and took the slaughtering knife and laid hold of his concubine and cut her up according to her bones into twelve pieces and sent her into every territory of Israel . . . Such a thing as this has never been brought about or been seen . . . Set YOUR hearts upon it, take counsel and speak."

—Judges 19:29, 30

we become what we live

so this act becomes
merely the story

men become one large phallus
towering into night

by rending garments and insides
hands become the fissure

torches   by being the sole
points of light   become stars

in the process of being broken
this sum becomes every broken body

by being flesh-gone   only
spirit   we are ever being

here and always here

*

There is no such work
as a woman's, a wife's, a concubine
by any other name.

These hands would settle sheep,
band cloth and hide, hem.
These hands held
water for desert thirst, held
barley, held.

O sons of the right hand,
sons of mourning, you know
these fingers, these joints.

Remember their trembling,
their stiffened grip
locked around the doorpost
as you loosened them, one nail,
one knuckle at a time.

*

"Honey comes in varying shades—from almost colorless to darker than molasses"

Our milk was sweet and dark, the color of honey.
That evening sky, the sun's low arc, the color of honey.

The long night's lamp: the sickle moon
sharp and stark, the color of honey.

The wheat in the harvest—its smooth stalks
bent then torn apart—the color of honey.

Afterbirth, the offspring that gave suck,
each stretch mark: the color of honey.

Our skin, and the men stripping it
like lotus bark, the color of honey.

A rite of Ba'al, this orgy. Daughters sent
through fire's spark, the color of honey.

The nameless face obscurity, like most rogues, most deities,
most left to the hull and bow of the ark, the color of honey.

*

In years before, we'd sojourn to the river when heat
gave way, our savior in drought or holy war.
On the path between penance and Lord's day
winds lifted the robe we wore, humming
songs of the ancients. We'd wade into water,
banishing filth and desire, letting
the swelling tide rise.

There in the alcove filled with brevity was providence—
the night fowls cleaning an opened deer—wild nature,
mortality. As the river billowed and ebbed,
overrun with moss and smoothstone,
the waiting mouth of the creek-bed
concealed the body with its drone—
this labyrinth music, nothing like home.

*

Say vulva and make it clean
say labia   say lips slip
        not folly   not force
or flinch   or fist

        Say clitoris and name it clean
say wet   not cyst   say slide
        not slight   not slash
not flay   not slit
        not splinter

        Say glans and claim it clean
say tip   say slick
        say graze   not gash
say trace   not bruise
        not mar   not wrest

                They
splay calves   under brush
                        fight to fill
        hollow   they scrape   they rip
        they scourge   they grip
say *open*   gape thighs
            then
                break them clean

*

"In the selfless abstractions their bodies became to the men who used them, they became more than 'sexual objects,' more even than mere women: they became 'Saints.'"

—Alice Walker

Women are burdened
with consequence

    hard-bought footprints
leading from each father's house

and this immaculate renewal, each season
the grass trampled

    by memory. Or worse, they bear
miraculous scars like Rita—patron saint

of difficult unions—who bore a prayer thorn
between temples and suffered

    foolishness, tyranny, at the hands
of offspring, all they bring.

When the saints took her body (before death,
in the interim between a kind of living)

    they gave the church no choice
and delivered her to the like-minded,

sisters of the faith. She told the unabridged story
then, robed among them,

    how he'd offered her up like sacrament,
how she prayed for the unthinkable:

before more harm, give death—
her own, his, idle sons'.

    Most women have no shrines,
they aren't idols, their piety

has not saved them.
Some are insufferable now,

    all around us,
their bodies made of east winds, their

branched and bulbed mouths.
Who can bear them

    when they take
to fields and pathways,

hewing their places among the reluctant—
truculent and double-tongued—

    desiring flesh
and damning it.

                    *

The bruise I can't remember is like the dream
of the woman's body: intact, whole.

I imagine the red welt
on my breast

is the body's pleading,
its landmark.

The woman reenters
almost as much as the quickened heartbeat

when I glance in the mirror.
She is splintered

battered, dark
like me, like my body.

She too returns to the house—
wearied, amnesic—

to lay what's left of her
down.

*

Don't birth us, Eve. We are clay and reed and sinew. We'll become Medusa. We'll bring everyone in. You'll try to bury us. Fix us to one place. Find some stone myth can't uncover. Name us or spit out what's left. We'll be the bludgeoned child, waking you. What meadowsweet will there be beneath us? Some voyagers pass through continents, others carry them, some never leave. Tethered to this life by what's missing, brought back into the belly. The choruses of hands, the red and reddening drums, how to raze them without fire? How to make this instrument a blooming, blazoned spire?

This is the worse kind of love story. Loving a thing to death, loving a thing until it strangles you. Doesn't that mean you hate us now—all you've inherited, all you'll become? Some breath is worth missing. This ugliness between us could be nothing. Who's to say our life wasn't typical? All our lives? Who says we'd need a rich man's well, something extraordinary, to hold all this water—the common wailing pieced together like a quilt? This could be punishment for lacking grace, not kneeling in prayer. Each morning we conjure a new excuse for the way we've been living. The stars have changed. Every few centuries they shift a bit. Transfixed on one that has dimmed and dimmed, we are looking, now, at kindling light, a blazing wick, the glow of a distant city.

*

We thought it would be
  a booming voice

but it's soft, smug like a lover
  saying I told you so.

It sounds like the key turning
  round a notch beyond

what was intended
  in the gate's worn lock.

When we ask, at first
  there is nothing.

The quiet means
  we're not through yet. When it comes

it is hungrier than we imagined,
  asking much back.

*

"Change is a fact of God."

　　　　　　—Grace Paley

I.

We are shimmering

the movement
around us
is not wind

the stones
anchoring our steps
are not cobblestones,

not meant
for the ever-traveling
heel

II.

　　　What holy number
　　　tallies *enough*?

III.

In this life
we were granted a name

it served us well:

midday we knelt
in prayer
for those
with hands full—

friends
who watched,
witnessed

IV.

Who sent us
        forward
or back?

Should we hail

        Yahweh
or Allah
        or Buddha
or Vishnu
        or Shaytan
or Olorun
        or Zeus
or Belial
        or Ra
or Melek Taus
        or Jesus
or Muhammad
        or Abraham
or
        Adam

as he is all we know

of divinity

V.

The woolgathering
is useful for shepherds

but this season
when the sheep are herded
into the pasture

let the call go out
among them early:

they are ripe

the garments
they'll harness

will not be thrown off
easily

VI.

One harvest, the fields we tended
went up in flames

dry season raked
the carob pods, the weeds,
the wheat

we lost oxen, large bodies
turned to ash
before planting,

sturdy horns—
charred and buried
whole—covered over
with singed earth and soot

we recall this reaping
when we are left to fire,

bare
in a field
outside the city,

burning
with the remains
of dogs

VII.

The next time
        we are sent to this earth
                we want no part of this body

the next time
        we want to live
                without consequence, with favor,
                        among men

the next time
        we are here, if we must be here,
                we want to remember
                        nothing

*

COME, came, comes, coming. v.

To return to a former position or state:
    "I came back to the meadow an unsuspecting hart, trying to wake up
        from a long night of/ walking"
    "if I came back as a bird/ I'd remember that"
    "no eternal fire,/ and no choosing what to come back as"
    "just as I am I come/ knee bent and body bowed"

To return, *esp.* to one's memory:
    "Every spring—/ Pilgrimage—the living come to mingle/ with the dead"
    "The flesh itself is finished/ so close it's come to the end/ of hunger,
        a husk set aside, tied shut"
    "What ghost comes to the bedside whispering *You?*"
    "It begins, it has an end/ this is what you will/ come back to"

To enter:
    "all the gods comin into me/ layin me open to myself"
    "You came up here with me/ with the voiceless/ thousands
        at the edge of the curtain"
    "I do not know where the words come from, what the millstones,
        where the turning may lead"
    "She is marvelous/ with waiting. Come. Hunt here./
        Relieve with hands and tongue her heavy hour"

To occur to the mind:
    "Their voices coming nearer, almost deciphered"
    "coming to/ the switchyard of the tongue"
    "who though they come to us/ From our own bodies/ Are altogether new"
    "above you/ another thing you couldn't possibly know was coming/
        another which, like your first breath, was not your idea"

To approach or move toward a particular person or place:
    "my comingback love"
    "An hour ahead of sun/ I come to find you. You're/ twisted

shut as a burr/ neck drooped unconscious"

"The process/ goes on forever: they come from sand/ they go back to gravel"

"they must come home yet again ashamed/ no matter where they have been"

To arrive by movement or in the course of progress:
"Unsown, it came fleshless, mud-ruddled, nothing/ but itself"
"the milk/won't come/the seed/won't plant/the womb
nulliparous/swells anyhow/"
"me and you/ coming from the same place"
"trust/ that what comes next comes after what came first./
She'll never be a story I make up"

To enter into being or existence; be born:
"I will leave understanding it/ was always coming; before that night,
even/ before we met"
"Come Armageddon, come fire or flood,/ come love, not love,
millennia of portents—"
"sooner or later the truth comes/ down heavy on every one of us"
"We'll come back/ Together at dawn/ And hate each other forever"

*

20

An incision in the neck allows for bleeding.
    Bless the soul leaving the body, bury the blood.

Cinnamon and myrrh preserve the dead; smear them with
    drops of perfumed oil from heel to temple.

Eye the markings of the bones, note their lay. Sharpen
    flint to shining.

Gather the hair and coil it.
    Handle the coarse length gently. Fasten with
ivory pins. Let none settle around the face.

    Judge the force it will take to sever
kin, this woman of your house. Hold each
    limb steady. Raise the blade.

Mourning women round the hearth.
    Night's cloak shrouding them, they raise a dirge.

Obscure the fragments: overlay the
    parcels with linen, then sackcloth, then wool.

Quell the blaze mounting your skin.
    Ready the horses, weigh them down with her.

Summon the messengers to the sanctuary.

    Tell them. Mete out the fractions
until you are cleansed of her. Call for
    vengeance, forgive her, her
wanderlust. Carry her history from Solomon to
    Xerxes, this time to that. Speak of what

you know: this is no myth.
    Zion was a witness. Journey home, let the body speak.

*

THINGS I CARRIED COMING INTO THE WORLD

The weight of my parents,
the dawn of them;
my grandmother's lackluster
life; the guilt of my grandfather's mistress
after he'd been scalded with hot
water, tender flesh boiling on his back;
my color, the umber slick of it
deepening over two weeks' time,
an aunt worrisome it would never stop;
the heart of a boy whose name
was forgotten before it was given
who passed me a note in fourth grade
that I spat upon and shot back
in scribbled, torn pieces;
obligation, the bane of memory,
the cleft a loss in 1967 creates
when a mother of mine
two mothers removed
is left broken on the sidewalk
after a drunk white man
jumps the curb
in the colored neighborhood,
the sorrow of the familiar voice
that has to tell me this;
my father's falsetto
before nicotine had its way
with his song; Jesus and all
his demands; soft hands;
the sight of a woman
at my first funeral, called away
to God, erupted, brought back
in a mega-church;

the bend of a slow, steady hump
overpowering an uncle's back;
my godson's vermillion face,
the uncertainty of him,
the walk I took with his mother,
past the clinic
through the divide;
a fistful of wanting; foreign bodies
wandering through my own;
a blow to the insides when distance
walks in; the braid of death,
streaked and ribboned against
my family's back, its greedy
interruption, its persistence,
the unwanted strands
of the thick-laced thing.

Maieusiophobia

My mother is unattainable
and I have come to accept this.
So when the doctor tells me—
my legs spread wide, the tiny head
of a probe invading my cervix—
There may be a problem
I am relieved, almost happy for the damage.
I say *Adoption is nice* randomly, to my mother,
driving through a flea market one day. Then
My students are all I need on another.
She watches me linger with children, then swiftly
hand them back, but never says what she intuits.
In the years to come I will say it outright:
I can't be you, meaning, not even one,
not even one perfect one.

What We Ask of Flesh

—for Jasmin Rae Francis

I.

IMPORTANT SAFEGUARDS

Close supervision is necessary when any appliance is used by children.

> A toddler is screaming
> and there is no other sound
> in the studio apartment
> on the wrong side of a dwindling city.

> This voice will ravage
> your sleep, for years,
> you will not be able
> to tame it.

> The room is full
> in some dreams. In others,
> there's only you,

> the absent mother, and the hands
> that lift the child from fire,
> even the scorched girl is barely there.

> This is how apparitions live—
> coming and going, rising
> and disappearing like smoke.

Extreme caution must be used when handling an appliance containing hot oil.

The pan is filled to the brim
and set on High (300 degrees).
When she steps, the child is immersed
in hot oil up to her ankles.

Liquid makes a trail from the foot
of the bed to the cracked tile,
past the TV, sullies an old towel, the lip
of the bathroom sink.

Do not use the appliance for other than intended use.

Her mother always begins the story
the same way

I was just trying to feed my kids,
we didn't have a stove

she calls on God, asks for help,
never mercy.

II.

The girl does not smile
in the portrait
of the grandchildren.

She cannot stand
and wears no shoes.
She stares into the camera

from a makeshift pedestal,
stoic, resembling the others.
Her bandaged feet swell

beneath the wool
someone has bought
to shield them.

Sapphire dye runs
by day's end, threatening
what must be clean:

the dressing's white linen,
regeneration, her rare blood—
backdrop of all within.

III.

INDEX

A

Adolescent search for self, *3*
Adoption of false self, *12*
Adult, child needs the same, *15*
Age most vulnerable, two to six, *23*
Anger, *32, 55, 60, 85, 92*
Attempt to make parent happy, *64*
Attempting the impossible, *65*

C

Child victim = adult victim, *91*
Children
      complying with madness, *67*
      parental fights, *66*
      role assigned before birth, *67*
Cultured skin, *25-26*

D

Depigmentation, *120*

H

Home, bedrooms, *162*;
      burn prevention in, *156*; children and,
      157-58, 160, 172, 173; electric
      supply, *165*; escape plans, *157*;
      flammable liquids, *172*; kitchens,
      158; living rooms, *162*; smoke
      detectors, *166*; smoking and

IV.

In the ruins, voices are one long-strung note:
    you hear the doctor
        Third degree   severe   ongoing trauma

then your grandmother, tending
    Let it breathe awhile
        don't wrap the skin so tight

In ten years, the girl will be
    taller than you
        and afraid of everything.

You offer
    Nobody's perfect
        I believe in mistakes

but time must pass
    before either of you
        accepts this.

When you ask
    what she recollects, she says
        I remember you there, then the ambulance

you pray on this
    recalling a lesson about sin:
        we are almost punishment enough for ourselves.

What is more blessed than forgiveness?
    a preacher asks, loud as the rustling pages
        What more could we ask of flesh?

V.

She coats her new skin
with shea butter and cotton

woven soft as gauze.
When you take her to the ocean

she wants to run along
the sand, *Like in the movies*

she says, but instead of baring
her body like other girls,

she shades what is
unforbidden, hollows

most often left to light.
She finds a jogging path

and stretches for mere seconds
before bolting out

onto the dunes.
In time, she returns complaining

that the land is unforgiving.
She is already weary

and has the whole shoreline to course.
She sits a bit defeated, near you,

cradling a shell in her hands.
It's harder than it looks, she says,

turning her back to the horizon
asking too much

How can we get anywhere
starting here?

and you must mention sunset
before she'll rise again.

VI.

salve, salved, salves, salvage. n. 1. A healing ointment for application to wounds: On third-degree burns, *salve* can only be applied after healing begins. 2. A remedy (*esp.* for spiritual disease): I wonder if God is a *salve*, can heal any wound? Some say, *Doubt is the Devil's trick.* I say, *I don't know him either. v.* 1. To anoint (a wound, wounded part) with a healing ointment: Bless the tender heels, bless the life lines reappearing, bless the brown turned black, turned back and turning, *salve* the rough skin and smooth. 2. To heal a person of sickness, sin, etc.: Years *salved* the time lost. I tested water, sand. I stretched leather again, I thinned lace. In due season, I walked. I ran. I leapt, stepped lightly. 3. To soothe, mitigate, assuage (an "appetite"): I crave this piecemeal mother of mine, want her as I've imagined: she'll return bearing her choices and I'll *salve* this hunger with questions she cannot answer. 4. A hypothesis that accounts for the motion of heavenly bodies: I am tectonic; nothing *salves* this shifting. I crash into myself, looking for some pulsing, a heartbeat, center, core. Watching the heavens, I find my portion weighed, unbalanced. 5. To save (property) from destruction by fire: That day I couldn't escape the fire, someone lifted me out. Someone carried me, some human or other being. I saw no clear face but heard many voices saying, *Live through this.* This blur, dim memories, most of what I have, I *salvage*.

VII.

USES FOR FIRE

ALTER: The flesh is lost after a burn
                    the heat can scar bone
             but   if it lives   it will heal

IGNITE: At the Homecoming Dance
                    the girl is a spark in the circling crowd

                    her hands flare
                    she wears no shoes

                    someone calls her name
                    but she is aflame with music

                    she does not stop, does not waste time
                    thinking of you or descent

                    there, reborn as celestial body—
                    more afterbirth than ash—

                    she makes a path
                    on the glittering floor

                    spinning wild and wide
                    while others follow

ILLUMINATE: Each time, you expect her to turn
                           to what you cannot know:

                    *Why were you there
                           that day? Why was I?*

                                  but she's learned some questions
                                  are better left to fire

INSPIRE: Hey love, hey child of mine, hey almost me, hey girl with a
             million questions, hey wunderkind, hey galaxy, hey voyager,
             hey sleuth, hey child who laughs at everything, hey child
             who's learned to laugh, hey trailblazer, hey heartbreaker, hey
             hip-shaker, hey pop-locker, hey hotshot, hey smooth, hey
             sweetest, hey here-today-grown-tomorrow, hey starshine, hey
             mystic, hey bright light, hey ember, *Hey Kid*, you say, just to
             hear her answer

PURIFY: When she is fifteen and ordinary
                     the girl calls to ask
                             about kissing

WORSHIP: Whether stones or coals or wood, the shallow
           trench tests purity, innocence, the roots,
           and those ablaze await

           recompense in this life or another.
           They carry on, glean
           their misfortunes, make the trek

           worthwhile. What most deem insufferable
           they count as blessing, proof of spirit,
           proof of flesh: they've learned

           we're given only what we need—
           ask for salvation and you're granted patience,
           ask for wisdom, peace comes to you,

           ask what's to follow and there stands
           the journey—uncharted, renewed

Nicole, Age Seven

—for Nicole Reid

Why he got you here
pretending to be human?
        Why he think we need
your hushed voice warning us
        that we can't answer
imperfection, can't tame it?

        Why he groom us
to let you go
        and why spirit got to be
barely a sprout, younger
        than most anything planted
in the harvest field,
        holding some spindle of autumn—
twigs and stems spun
        olive or golden or auburn—
in her hands?

        Why send something more fragile
than iceglass or worn sheets?
        Why kindle
your plain logic—put it in your heart
        to sit near picture windows
when storms rise, call the ancestors
        claiming them, whispering everything
most won't hear—all the world
        and all that frightens me in it?

Why he got to make sure we know
        we're a stone's throw
from oblivion, reminding us

every time you turn our corner,
God so big
even his smallest things
sparkle like a million
silver coins?

KUPERBERG, SOUTH SIDE STREET PHOTO

The little boy in Anna's photo
shines like the little boy
we've been searching for,
found last night in the last place
we wanted him: the backseat
of the white truck, shell
casings littering the floor.
In the photo, he is watching
for someone outside the shot,
his mouth full with sugary sweet
eaten whole, only the stick
poking through pursed lips.
His eyes are wide.
In the truck, the boy's eyes
are perpetually wide.
The children in the photo are perched
on a stoop, not far
from the stoop where the boy
in the truck used to play tag and hunt,
chase girls with unraveling
plaits, like the girl behind the boy
in the photo. The boy
in the truck could have been
the boy taken in a flash.
But time is only still here,
in the photo, no one captures
the uncertain space
behind the waiting door.

III.

All the Wild Swarm

On Three Creeks Road
past the prison and small inlets
the church seems a long way off

as the funeral line turns
down the drive, not far
from the congregation of sandstone

in the field.
What hovers there
is not only spirit

but hundreds, maybe thousands,
of carpenter bees—
their striped bodies

dimming the tower,
its ducts blooming
with honey and hives.

Their shimmer akin
to dusk light, and their sound
the low murmur of a rising flock.

Myths say they are what's left
of the body, born of entrails
or tears. Here, they amass

near everything not resting
and brush my cheek
as I move up the dirt path,

arms filled
with a heavy wreath,
fragrant and rife with nectar.

The horde of bees
trails the procession,
messengers

sent to worry
each body, serving
as shadowland bridge,

moving past history
to the open plot
where the blossoms

come to rest,
where all the wild swarm
soon will.

SOMETHING DIVINE LET GO

Even the poor
know that richness,
the fragrance of the lemon trees

   —Eugenio Montale

We opened
two halves
of a miracle

   —Pablo Neruda, "Ode to the Lemon"

Free groves spread out
over miles of dirt road

and my grandmother—
astonished at the sight

of the vast orchard
with lemons large enough

to eclipse her palm—
led us in among the fruit

through shadows, past
bouquets of leaves and blossoms,

until day yielded to evening
and the limbs she bent

were bare.
Carrying citrus home,

we sliced the bright bodies,
added pulp and rind to sugar, water,

black dime-store tea.
By sunset, we welcomed grace:

hands sifting creation,
small gifts, filling our space.

*

When she died, memory
mounted the table, incense filled the house.

Folks spoke of bread pudding and scratch biscuits,
then of how home was bittersweet—

the mistress creeping back to the back door
after granddaddy was laid to rest,

weary Sundays when dirt or blood
marred the thin linens she pressed.

One knew of our matriarch
offering lemons after salvaging

a basket full, a bit tender
but not waste, aged and softened

but still good.
A storeowner let her take all

she wanted, in his hurry
to make way for new

and my grandmother comforted
the downtrodden—a woman

who must have resembled
herself, sitting near the window, shut-in

aged and ailing,
watching for what wouldn't soon come.

She soothed her, bearing fruit,
said it didn't take much

to find a reason to live.
Told her just sit on the porch

in daylight, let the sun worry
and spread the slices thin.

Turn the alms over in her hands,
savoring them, let God settle in.

House of the Ten Plagues

"Sometimes we call God the Devil."

—Kevin Simmonds

1.

I should be Moses

but I am Pharaoh
in this house

faucets run red
the week I arrive

some say rust,
some fear blood,

all say *It will come to pass*

2.

The value will double
this from the realtor as I scan documents,
sign. There's water behind, off to the east.
Maybe mosquitoes, a frog or two,
some flooding but *don't worry*
you'll get it all back.

3.

The fruit bears gnats.
The plants bear gnats.
They bloom,
like the buds that bring them,
they are revenant.
They bear fruit.
They rise out of dust.

4.

When the gadflies come
I am still obstinate.

I will not leave or plead
even when they make their task clear:

they're here for blood.
They fill my shower

with slender, silver wings.
Their eyes shimmer as they wait for me.

I am marked by the beasts,
their bites like omens;

the skin they taint left
swollen and inflamed. What remains,

after clearing the house
of clutter and waste, is the flesh

they crave. They need
the living body as prey.

Before they depart
at least they're candid,

It's not your fault, they say,
Your God is hungry, and must be fed.

5.

On occasion, I find a carcass:
a robin, a mouse, a squirrel,
but the bodies grow in spring.
One morning the vestige of a cat appears.
Two mornings later, at the foot of my driveway,
I swerve to miss what's left of a missing dog.

6.

My doctor has become a priest:
It's stress he says *you're under pressure*

These sores will heal themselves
Give them time

They're spreading I say

No believe me
that's all in your mind

7.

Cedarwood transfigures in the storm.
      Every year when nor'easters form, swarming
      the coast, bringing rain and wind and sometimes
thunder, the deck out back holds all that's left

behind: tree limbs, beach grit, stones, and enough
      damp seed that birds come, featherslick and fixed
      on salvaging their harvest. This fall,
there's fury. And I recall the quarter-sized

ice coating what's lost to us now:
      the deck of the house on that new country road,
      pressed pinewood and Georgia red brick. My parents
led us to the sliding glass doors and we watched

the downpour. Didn't imagine, then, we'd
      stand witness to the end of it all, every
      piece lost or repossessed. For all we know,
there's, more or less, nothing left but memory

and what's sent: the lightning meant to warn me
      that everything we touch can fade away—
      notches in the wood where hailstones shatter,
the fallen posts, a burning bush, all remnants—nothing stays.

8.

Countless bodies in the tub
don't drown and won't be caught.
The exterminator calls them large outdoor roaches,
this is their breeding ground: low house,
over the sewer drain, vacant for years.
No matter how clean you've been
he says, spraying poison behind the mirror,
under the sink, on the bleached baseboards,
as long as you're on earth
they'll find a way in.

9.

I am baptized near the winter solstice.

It has been months since the curses set in
and I no longer fear what I can't control.

The lights have died. I gather
candles and pray

until sleep comes
and nothing stirs.

10.

I'm sure by now I've killed it.
Firstborn blood runs
past my thighs.

I am not careful.
I do not count days.

When men come
I am not merciful.
I leave the doorway bare.

　　　What good could it do
to yield now

when someone has already
claimed the ground?

WILL AND TESTAMENT

Strip the pictures from the walls.
Send these with me.

I won't be able to open my eyes
if they are sewn shut

but I may be able to feel, to patch
the decomposing pieces when I am called to wake.

Cremate me. Do it quickly, without fanfare,
unless this troubles my mother.

If she can't stand the thought of not seeing me
slick and stiff in a prettied-up box,

give her what she wants;
even in death there are sacrifices.

If there is marching down to the family plot,
I'd like to be with Grandmama,

near Granddaddy, at the edge
of the cemetery by the highway

off Grace Street, as good a place
as any to lie.

Once my uncle has spun a seasoned prayer,
I want the road trod back with Bomba and brass,

percussion and pyre; trust the wind
to wind up bodies and hands to spark fire.

Send up celebration: marching song wide
with arc and bellow—feathered hats lifted,

      handkerchiefs waving then cast away—
      a bittersweet opus, clamor and revelry

      carrying me from the long road
      of the boneyard city,

      past Mama, past grace, on through
      to any other side.

How I Crossed Over

I. Clifton

most wonder
whether the foxes
warned me

if my twelve
fingers   threaded
to past and future
twitched   when
the journeymen came

but some know

signs are for those
not made
of spirit

i woke
unmarked
bearing familiar
wings

II. Ai

I know the Rider better than others—his cloak
like sackcloth, stiff and thick as an abductor's cape—
but they all greet me to pay homage:

Hades, rich with invisibility
Osiris, reassembled, returning
Lucifer, with his clear music

even the forgotten and unutterable
thank me for bearing their children,
naming them and giving voice.

They nod recalling our offspring—
wife-murderers, child-beaters,
cannibals—hearkened to light.

Draping me in violet, they plead
but I want silence
lining the broad way.

I am gracious, disappearing,
as they beckon   *Sweet Medium,*
who'll flicker? Who'll flame?

III. Rodgers

When mama enters this time
she is like the old insurance man
with her checks and balances

she inspects the house and tallies
what I haven't done—

      no savings

           no spare rooms

                no Bible worn thin

she licks the tip of her pen
like old folks do,
to mark me, mark what's missing,
but nothing comes

Here I say *I have a way*
with these things

the ink flows
heavy as blood
when I press against
the ledger

and mama watches,
waits to see if
all that truth tellin'
gon' hold
through to the afterlife

I finish her work:

      no companion

           no assets anyone can see

mama shakes her head like a southside preacher,
      summons

Child, cross ovah here wit' me

So I become
my blinding self:

black bird
singing:

home, free

NOTES

The book's opening quote is from Lucille Clifton's poem "dear fox" from *The Terrible Stories* (1996).

"The Body Speaks" is based on an account from the book of Judges, Chapter Nineteen, in which a visiting woman is raped by a mob of townsmen. The woman dies shortly thereafter and, upon finding her, the woman's husband cuts her into pieces and sends her body parts into each of the twelve tribes of Israel. The biblical verses cited are from the *New World Translation of the Holy Scriptures,* published by the Watch Tower Bible and Tract Society of New York, Inc. (1984).

The third section of the poem contains an epigraph from Janet Raloff's article "The Color of Honey" published in *Science News* (1998).

The sixth section of the poem contains an epigraph from Alice Walker's essay "In Search of Our Mothers' Gardens" from her book of the same title (1983).

In April 2007, Du'a Khalil Aswad, a seventeen-year-old member of a minority Kurdish religious group called Yezidi, was killed in an "honor killing" due to her alleged relationship with a Sunni Muslim boy. Men from her family and town stoned her to death while others recorded the incident with cell phones. The tenth section of the poem is based on this event. This section contains an epigraph from Grace Paley's short story "Goodbye and Good Luck" from *The Little Disturbances of Man* (1959).

The eleventh section of the poem is made up almost entirely of lines from the following poems or works, most of which were found on the Academy of American Poets website (www.poets.org), and are listed in the order in which they appear: Elizabeth Willis, "The Steam Engine"; Ellen Bryant Voigt, "Practice"; Maxine Kumin, "In the Park"; Harryette Mullen, "Muse & Drudge [just as I come]"; Natasha Trethewey, "Pilgrimage"; Rebecca Wee, "Uncertain Grace"; Carolyn Forché, "Sequestered Writing"; Margaret Atwood, "You Begin"; Ntozake Shange, "for colored girls who have considered suicide/ when the rainbow is enuf"; Dana Levin, "In the Surgical Theatre"; Jane Hirshfield, "Waking the Morning Dreamless After Long Sleep"; Lisa Russ Spaar, "After John Donne's 'To His Mistress Going to Bed'"; Judy Jordan,

"Help Me to Salt, Help Me to Sorrow"; Emily Wilson, "Pastoral"; Anne Porter, "Noël"; Catherine Doty, "Momentum"; Dana Goodyear, "Séance at Tennis"; May Swenson, "Little Lion Face"; Amy Clampitt, "Beach Glass"; Jorie Graham, "Nearing Dawn"; Claudia Emerson, "Bone"; Carol Moldaw, "The Lightning Field, 6"; Lucille Clifton, "sisters"; Marilyn Hacker, "Nearly a Valediction"; Andrea Werblin, "Barrio with Sketchy Detail"; Eleanor Lerman, "The Mystery of Meteors"; Honorée Fanonne Jeffers, "At the Shelter"; and Gwendolyn Brooks, "Callie Ford."

"Nicole, Age Seven" is written after August Wilson's play *Joe Turner's Come and Gone* (1998).

"House of the Ten Plagues" opens with an epigraph from a phone conversation with the poet Kevin Simmonds. The italicized lines in the fourth section of the poem are from E.L. Voynich's novel *The Gadfly* (2003).

"Something Divine Let Go" takes its title and epigraph from Eugenio Montale's poem "The Lemon Trees" from *Montale in English* (2004).

A Note on the Author

REMICA L. BINGHAM, a native of Phoenix, Arizona, is an alumna of Old Dominion University and Bennington College as well as a Cave Canem Fellow. Her first book, *Conversion* (Lotus Press, 2007), won the Naomi Long Madgett Poetry Award and was short-listed for the Hurston/Wright Legacy Award. She resides with her husband and children in Norfolk, Virginia. For more information on her work and upcoming events, visit www.remicalbingham.com.

Books from Etruscan Press

White Vespa | Kevin Oderman
The Shyster's Daughter | Paula Priamos
Saint Joe's Passion | JD Schraffenberger
Lies Will Take You Somewhere | Sheila Schwartz
Fast Animal | Tim Seibles
American Fugue | Alexis Stamatis
The Casanova Chronicles | Myrna Stone
The White Horse: A Colombian Journey | Diane Thiel
The Fugitive Self | John Wheatcroft

Etruscan Press Is Proud of Support Received From

Wilkes University

Youngstown State University

The Raymond John Wean Foundation

The Ohio Arts Council

The Stephen & Jeryl Oristaglio Foundation

The Nathalie & James Andrews Foundation

The National Endowment for the Arts

The Ruth H. Beecher Foundation

The Bates-Manzano Fund

The New Mexico Community Foundation

The Gratia Murphy Endowment

Founded in 2001 with a generous grant from the Oristaglio Foundation, Etruscan Press is a nonprofit cooperative of poets and writers working to produce and promote books that nurture the dialogue among genres, achieve a distinctive voice, and reshape the literary and cultural histories of which we are a part.

etruscan press
www.etruscanpress.org

Etruscan Press books may be ordered from

Consortium Book Sales and Distribution
800.283.3572
www.cbsd.com

Small Press Distribution
800.869.7553
www.spdbooks.org

Etruscan Press is a 501(c)(3) nonprofit organization.
Contributions to Etruscan Press are tax deductible
as allowed under applicable law.
For more information, a prospectus,
or to order one of our titles,
contact us at books@etruscanpress.org.